MW01254227

The Egg Mistress

Poems
Jessica Poli

Book design by Joseph Kaplan
Gold Line Press logo by Nicholas Katzban

Gold Line Press publishes chapbooks of poetry and fiction
with the aim to promote the work of emerging writers as
well as showcase the chapbook form. The goal of our annual
competition is to support exceptional writers through the
publication and broad distribution of their work. Gold Line
Press is associated with the University of Southern California's
Ph.D. program in Literature and Creative Writing.

ISBN 978–1-938900–03–7

Library of Congress Control Number: 2013933001

Gold Line Press

3501 Trousdale Parkway, THH 431 Los Angeles, CA 90089-
0354 www.goldlinepress.com

The Egg Mistress

poems
JESSICA POLI

Acknowledgments

Poems within this book have first appeared in the following publications: *The Camel Saloon, Collision Literary Magazine, The Dirty Napkin, elimae, > kill author, Monongahela Review, red lightbulbs, Revolution House, Santa Clara Review, Sixth Finch, South Dakota Review,* and *Utter Magazine.*

Many thanks to Gold Line Press and Mark Irwin for making this book a reality. Special thanks goes to the lovely Portia Elan for the title "The Bodies We Make for Ourselves Are the Bodies We Desire," as well as to the 3-4-5 writing community for always being there.

Also and forever, thanks and love to my family and friends, especially my parents, who have always been supportive and loving.

Table of Contents

Origin of South

There is a lake coming.
And under it, the idea of church.

In a room somewhere, the cat starts singing.
I catch birds in my mouth. I say without saying:

Look at the lake. The way it looks—
unlost. The way bottles look

upside down. The spin of trap doors.
The way planets and bodies of water

tend to dance. You and I
dancing in the cotton, where what-ifs crop.

If I could speak mineral.
If I could only eat bonemeal. If the cabbage

learned not to grow roots. If you were the barn
and I was the peeled corn.

Lunch and Love in the Cottage

I hang cotton dresses
on a line of hot nitrogen.
Our day is aired and new,
the seams invisible.

I wash the butter knife
for the mangoes you devour from the garden,
eat thorns with raspberry jam
scooped into silver spoons.

Early in our morning, a pair of iodine lips
whispered against shaking knees.
You hung across the bed
like cloth along the clothesline.

After we make love, I run to turn the faucet off.
Kitchen sink overflowing, water and thorns
spilling onto bleached tile.
You walk into the flood and fill a cup.

Extraction

1
I have salted my teeth.
Now the tide of sucking in/the water pouring
out. The commotion in between is
breathtaking, my head full of some sort of geranium
dance. The blood is significant
but we can come to it later.

2
I am watching flowers
burst from your ears. Too engrossed to notice
the house going up in flames behind me,
although I know somehow the exposed beams
resemble your legs. There is something to say
about water, how it comes and goes.

3
My teeth erupt from their sockets as
the flowers are picked. Or maybe plucked. I will only
let go when I learn that I will never let go.
There is something to be said
about water laced with blood. The beams were shaking
just like your legs.

The Bodies We Make for Ourselves
Are the Bodies We Desire

This is how we dance: pulling lettuce out of the soil
by its dirty roots. Grabbing panties from the clothesline.

You call my eyes *dead blue*. You swear
my pulse runs at an angle.

We watch what falls off the bed: good intentions,
a collection of spoons, and endless strings.

I catch you making spiders dance.
Find you with scissors and too much hair.

You should know, as I fold the dirty sheets
along the longitude of our sweat,

that I'm a believer now.
And that this body holds beating.

And that I am still alone and still too young
to be as naked as you've made me.

Blackberry Picking After Old Michaelmas

Winter fell in a heap.
Not snow—dark mud,
stiff molding grass.

Roots couldn't last here.
I became deaf. Berry bushes died.
The last rush of the river pulled us under

before we could scream.
We chewed on seeds while we drowned.

The Egg Mistress

In the morning, I fill the counter with crab legs.
Large white pots boil on the stovetop
ready for an afternoon feast.

I keep my hands full.

Pass your name with salt over burners.

In the kitchen, there are two of myself—
one cooking, stirring, sautéing,
one lying dead on the slick tile,
crabs crawling and tangling in her hair.

I step over her and fry an egg.

I Hide the Core Heap Under the Bed

Balsa hands and
red sugar on hot fingers:
you used to have a hold on me.

We loved caffeine and
made love under black lights,
teeth glowing as they crashed together.

Lint from the dryer
tends to settle on my lips. Remember,
you used to brush it away. Used to call me things.

I've been a lot of things—
sea monsters and bridesmaids.
You said them all while you traced my thighs.

Let me melt, I always said.
You fed me apples in the morning.
You told me not to cry and fed me apples.

With Dysthymia

comes the loss of blood weight.
The bride spat. We like bones, here. We like birds.

Under the tent, foxgrape climbing empty tables.
Bride splitting almonds with bleeding teeth.

In my hand, an artichoke I'll slice eventually. A knife
tucked somewhere into something to be driven into

something else. The slaughter later—
for now, we rest.

We don't know how long we've been here
but the ground is starting to give way.

Blues for Wednesday

Wednesday came with a sigh
and we raised our arms mechanically
for our shirts to be lifted,
blue cotton falling.

Place us
on the Formica kitchen counter
beside oranges, point our toes
toward tile, sea green linoleum.

ihearyoushhh.

A white parakeet you held at the zoo.
My memory of tortilla chips,
grease and salt.
The black gurgle of the coffee maker.

In the morning I felt you turn away.
I woke up with leaves in my bed,
not your breath.
Like autumn spilling into my sheets.

What's underneath is gone,
a peach-silk slip crumpled on the floor,
a dress
deflated and wanting.

Beds arrange themselves
in every corner of my head.
Lay down: our pulses granite
and blues and shades of the radio.

We're too grown and love too little.
I watched you climb a tree—
dead eggs inside a bird's nest,
they were blue blue blue.

The Cream Mistress

Here is the girl you don't love,
naked, walking to buy cream,
crossing roads and alleys here
and here, passing wild onions
there in a patch.

A bride in your bed at noon,
she's waking you like this and
like this, she's slicing apples in
your kitchen for your children
for their lunches.

Here she is undone under you,
blue dress and parted legs like
this, and like this, thin-skinned,
twisting and arching and there
for your reaping.

Here is this girl bringing you
cream and coffee after waking,
saying Baby I love you, Baby,
in this rhythm that you know,
that you should love, that you
only tolerate.

Here is your lover you never
love, who crowns you every
evening lying down, her love
falling from the bed, slipping
through floorboards.

The Title of This Poem Is Something Sad

Sarah says she will show me how *not to need* and I think this
is great until she starts removing furniture from her ribcage.
She tells me she is the word *excavation*. Or maybe it was
evacuation. Splitting is something we have always done to
pass the time. If we were animals, she'd be a jackal and I'd be
an egg. On my grocery list I write *free range chicken* but end
up buying beef. Here are some truths: I am a collection of
almosts. Sarah will give birth to a beautiful boy who will die
in his sleep. There is a place underneath the riverbed where
none of this is real.

Origin of Empty Places

In the hallway closet I keep dresses that won't fit until my next relationship. I'll bring them with me when I move. The bottles that litter the floor can stay, let them think what they will. Sometimes I slide against the laminate floor and beg it to hold me. The nature of radiators is to cry and cry. The sound of my neighbors having sex reminds me of antlers scraping against the hood of a car. In rhythm with their creaking I say *zero, zero, zero*. I am always buying bottles of nothing and attempting to empty them. When I'm saddest, I read *Vogue*. I mourn over my naked fingernails. I've been here before; I recognize the stairs. The house is a tangle of paint and tongues.

The Rapture

We were tangled like fish.
The marionette keened from its place on the desk,
just like us. Just like the bed creaking.
Lonely, we twisted together under what I wished was heat
while you wished I was her.

The land there doesn't love. It thunders,
a jhanic flood, makes the body jump to the sky.
Explodes within and churns us in waves.
On the side of a mountain, I trailed blood along rocks.
The mosquitoes hovered, their wings
grown old before they did, and we paused.

And when the sky broke in half
you weren't there to see it, and I wasn't surprised.

Diagram

I have said all the wrong things.
I thought he would peel me open

like an orange,
split the rind, thick

epicarp stripped, shuck this
raw husk to see what's

underneath, high in tannins
& other polyphenols—I'd die

& dye, dour milkglass mouth
pressed to mine. I know in the light

of anatomy & morning
that we weren't anything,

white thigh against milk-
white thigh; no atria involved.

I have split myself in two &
found nothing. I have halved

the single cell where I thought
we kept our ventricles, but

it only spilled dissolved molecules
that might have been

part of a hand or some absent
organ, & I have diagrammed

it all to remember every way
a body can be stripped.

The Naming of Things Kept Us Busy

landlocked | deadbolt | dust bowl | house in the middle. We read the entire list at the ceremony. After all, we were so careful about getting everything right, stuck on the word *love* for a day—love, like the failure of the word *lung*, like mineral. A grassy kiss against teeth. Grinning badly by a cactus. The blood dog's bite against your thigh. Finally we settled: a hand in a room full of hands.

Look Out

I try and make my eyes say *let's see how long we can kiss* but you don't read eye-language so we don't kiss at all. Your eyes say *Let's wear out the soles of our feet then buy new ones.* They say *Let's go to the carnival and light fires beside every popcorn stand.* In this one scenario, you're holding a bird cage and when you open it the room smells like cinnamon and I laugh and I laugh and we dance. My eyes say HEAT. They say LOOK OUT. You and I are trapped in the carnival with heat and nothing else between us. There is nothing between us. I'm still trying to wrap my hand around yours but a carnival monkey runs over and chews it off. I eat popcorn until I explode.

Dream In Which Everything Is Untitled

The warp and woof of piano keys keeps me up at night.

Suddenly I wonder if I can even have children, and my bedroom
windows are open and not open, and I am here and not here. I am

bleeding and not bleeding.

I thought the cotton grew in the kitchen.
I thought we would always grow.

I thought we could sew the carrots to our fingers raw.

The Barn

I go there now, walk on
molding feathers,
dead hen in the corner.
Where we held sweaty hands
and pushed together foreheads.
The room where I undressed,
where beside sacks of flour
and creased Bible pages
I curled my new and unused body
around yours. Where I shed
a teaspoon of blood
now dried on floorboards.
Where without reservation
you peeled me like the rind
of an unripe fruit, gnats and
barnflies working their way
between our torsos.
I know now that things die.
A rotting hen told me.
Said, from the corner of the room:
You know you'll have to start over.
The deadbolt isn't thrown
(my fingers too sore, too stiff)
but it won't matter, you'll
never try to get in again. The
barn will stay quiet and rot,
and I will listen to the mold of that hen
and stand in a hot steaming room,
in light that comes through
dirty dishes and perfume, and
remove myself
to boil in clouded water

and add spines, vertebrae,
scraps for a new body
drawn up over breakfast
including a detailed map
of every artery and vein
and every inch of my skin
that wouldn't have been touched by you.

Detritus

1

I threw away cranberries—trash can full
of eggshells and coffee, now smeared red.
And over it all, I threw salt.
Pulled myself under sheets and left the mess for Monday.

2

When I left, wet snow was muffling the sound of cranes
tearing down the hospital.
I heard it muting down Atwood Street.
A block and then twelve and the sound died but the
ground still shook.

3

"I don't know if I can love like that again."
She said it and threw salt in her mouth.

4

Mess still heavy when I came back; cranberries rotted.
It would all turn into great hills—
crows hanging above it from strings,
dipping toward the garbage heap.
Everyone would come to see.

24

The gulls still chase me,
heavily. Teeth battered.

In between
my mouth rearranging itself
and you asking what's wrong,

I softly explode like soda
opened underwater.

Things I remain certain of include
the cancer I will someday have
and you.

Lately, I keep windows open
and hope for birds to fly in. I grind teeth

down to nothing. Picture the daughters
we might have had. Envy the sofa
she sits on now.

The barn still swallows me,
and I still come to it unyielding.

Jessica Poli grew up in Ligonier, Pennsylvania, but also calls Pittsburgh her hometown. She is currently studying in the MFA program at Syracuse University, and is editor of the online magazine *Birdfeast*.

SELF-PORTRAIT